THE STORY OF
Saint Patrick

A story of unselfish devotion

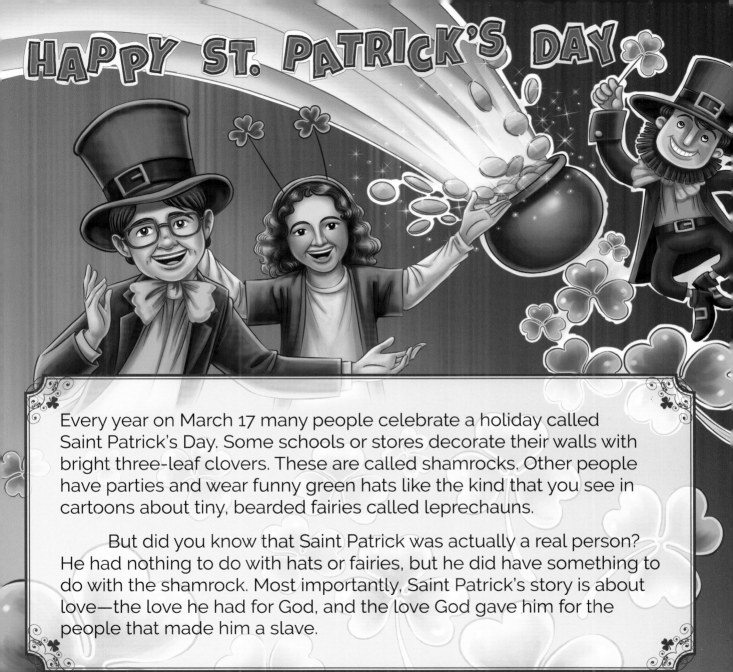

Every year on March 17 many people celebrate a holiday called Saint Patrick's Day. Some schools or stores decorate their walls with bright three-leaf clovers. These are called shamrocks. Other people have parties and wear funny green hats like the kind that you see in cartoons about tiny, bearded fairies called leprechauns.

But did you know that Saint Patrick was actually a real person? He had nothing to do with hats or fairies, but he did have something to do with the shamrock. Most importantly, Saint Patrick's story is about love—the love he had for God, and the love God gave him for the people that made him a slave.

It was a peaceful night.

17-year-old Patrick made himself comfortable in his soft, fluffy bed. The crackling fire gave the room a golden glow and the sounds of the ocean waves outside were gently lulling him to sleep.

He had just shut his eyes when he heard loud shouting and noises outside. Wondering what the clamor was, he sat up. Just at that moment, his father rushed into the room.

"Patrick!" he shouted. "We are being attacked, and you must escape!"

Before he knew it, his father was pushing him towards an open window. "Run! Quickly—RUN!" his father shouted.

Patrick landed on the ground with a thud and then did as he was told. He ran. He ran through the garden. He ran as fast as he could. Until—

"Got you!"

Patrick felt two strong arms grab his shoulders. Looking up, he was face to face with a wild, rugged man.

"Put him with the others!" the man ordered, and Patrick was taken away.

Patrick groaned as he was tossed into the hold of a large ship. It was dark, but he could tell that he was not alone.

"What's to become of us?" a man cried out.

Patrick looked around. The man was bound with chains, as were the other people in the hold. He recognized some of them. He had seen them in the village.

"What's happening?" Patrick whispered. "Who are these people and why are they treating us this way?"

"They are savage Irishmen!" one of the men in chains replied. "And now we are their prisoners."

Soon Patrick was bound with the other captives and the ship set out to sea. It was a long night for Patrick. He thought about his family, and he wondered if he would ever see them again.

"Get up!"

Patrick woke up from a sound sleep. His arms hurt, and then he remembered why.

"Welcome to Ireland!" one of the wild men jeered as the prisoners were pushed out of the ship. "This is now your new home!" he added with a cruel laugh.

Patrick looked around at the countryside. It was green and beautiful, but he had little time to enjoy the view. Before Patrick knew it, he had been sold to a farmer as a slave!

As they made their way to his master's house, Patrick looked around. It was a very strange country that he had been taken to. He could see many altars to pagan gods along the way.

"May God in heaven help us!" one of the prisoners whispered to him. "These people are very superstitious. They believe in many strange gods, and from what I hear, they offer cruel sacrifices to them!"

All that Patrick heard and saw made him very scared.

"You'll take care of my sheep!" the farmer shouted to Patrick, as they got to the farm. "And make sure you don't lose one of them or you'll feel my whip at your back!"

From that day on, Patrick spent long hours in the countryside taking care of sheep and sometimes doing hard work on the farm. His master was cruel and treated him harshly. It was a life that Patrick was not used to.

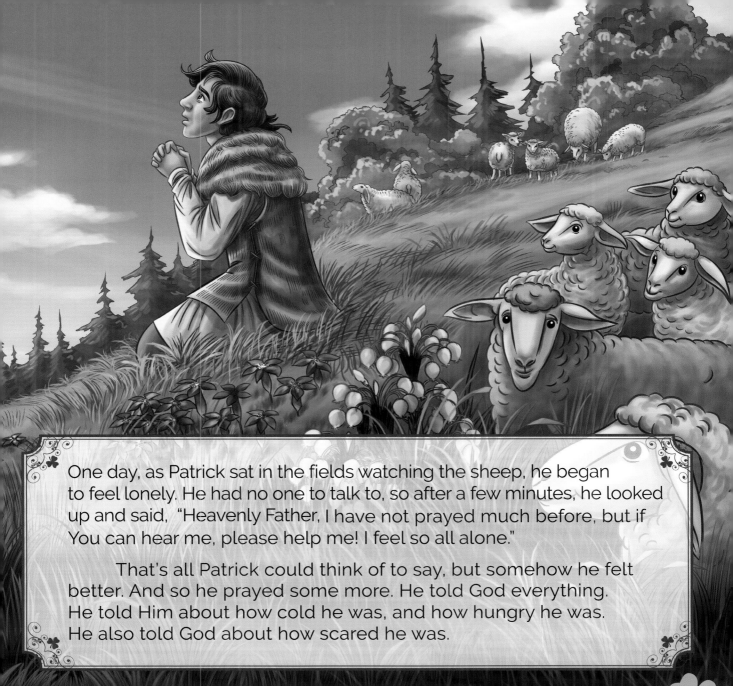

One day, as Patrick sat in the fields watching the sheep, he began to feel lonely. He had no one to talk to, so after a few minutes, he looked up and said, "Heavenly Father, I have not prayed much before, but if You can hear me, please help me! I feel so all alone."

That's all Patrick could think of to say, but somehow he felt better. And so he prayed some more. He told God everything. He told Him about how cold he was, and how hungry he was. He also told God about how scared he was.

The more he prayed, the better he felt, so as the days went by, Patrick continued to pray.

When he thought of his parents, Patrick prayed, "Dear God, please bless my parents. Please keep them safe and give them comfort when they miss me." When he thought about being a slave, he would say, "Dear Jesus, You see I am a slave now and how hard it is. Please free me!"

Soon Patrick was speaking to God about everything and, as a result, his heart began to fill with joy. He started thanking God for the beautiful sunsets and the funny sheep, the soft grass and the refreshing water. Sometimes he would just thank God for being there with him. Patrick began to share every moment with God, and the more he did, the closer he felt God's presence.

"God is wonderful!" Patrick would tell the other slaves. "If you pray and tell Him your troubles, He will help you, too!"

Some of the men would make fun of Patrick. "Being with the sheep all day is making you crazy!" they laughed. "If God is so wonderful, why are we still prisoners?"

Patrick learned not to let their words bother him. He just kept on praying. He was at peace with God.

Several years passed. One night, as Patrick slept, he had a strange dream: a man stood on the shore, pointing to a boat.

"This is the ship that will take you home," the man said to Patrick. "It is waiting for you! It is waiting!"

Patrick woke up with a start. *Could God be speaking to me through this dream?* he thought to himself.

As the days passed, Patrick could not get the dream out of his mind, so he prayed that God would show him what to do.

Convinced that the dream was direction from God, a few nights later, he quietly picked up his belongings and slipped out of the camp.

Patrick had escaped.

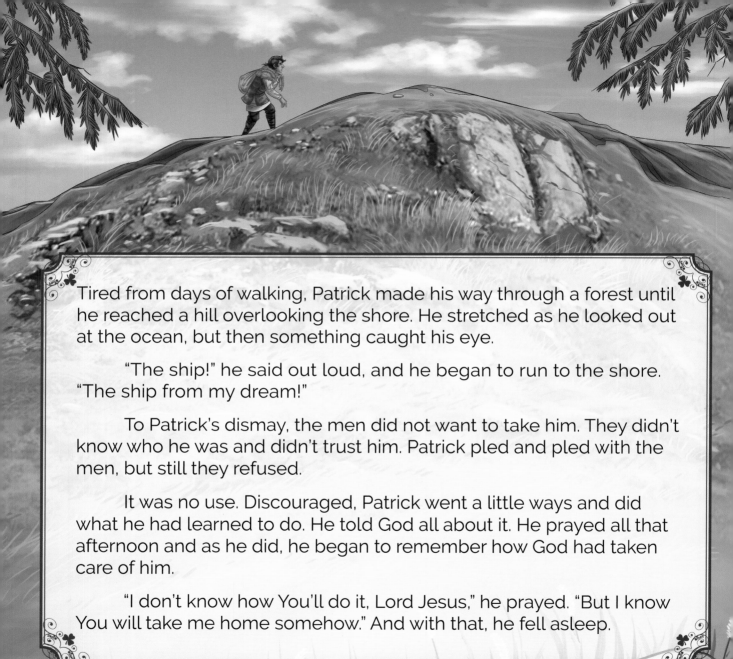

Tired from days of walking, Patrick made his way through a forest until he reached a hill overlooking the shore. He stretched as he looked out at the ocean, but then something caught his eye.

"The ship!" he said out loud, and he began to run to the shore. "The ship from my dream!"

To Patrick's dismay, the men did not want to take him. They didn't know who he was and didn't trust him. Patrick pled and pled with the men, but still they refused.

It was no use. Discouraged, Patrick went a little ways and did what he had learned to do. He told God all about it. He prayed all that afternoon and as he did, he began to remember how God had taken care of him.

"I don't know how You'll do it, Lord Jesus," he prayed. "But I know You will take me home somehow." And with that, he fell asleep.

"Wake up!"

Patrick opened his eyes to see the captain of the ship.

"I don't know why I'm doing this, but I've changed my mind and we are leaving now. If you want to come with us, you can!"

A few minutes later Patrick was on the ship. "I'm going home!" he shouted. "God has freed me from being a slave, and I am going home!"

"It's my boy! My boy is alive!"

Patrick's mother could hardly believe her eyes. Hearing her cries, Patrick's father also ran out of the house and soon all three were hugging and thanking God.

"This is a miracle!" his mother said. "We thought we would never see you again!"

Soon Patrick was enjoying all the comforts of home. He had his own room, clean clothes, and a loving family and friends. He quickly forgot his life as a slave, but he did not forget God.

"Lord Jesus," he prayed. "You took care of me when I was all alone. You showed me what to do. Help me to stay close to You always!"

Patrick was now home. He was no longer a teenager. He was a young man. His time in Ireland had been very hard, but in his difficulty, Patrick had found God.

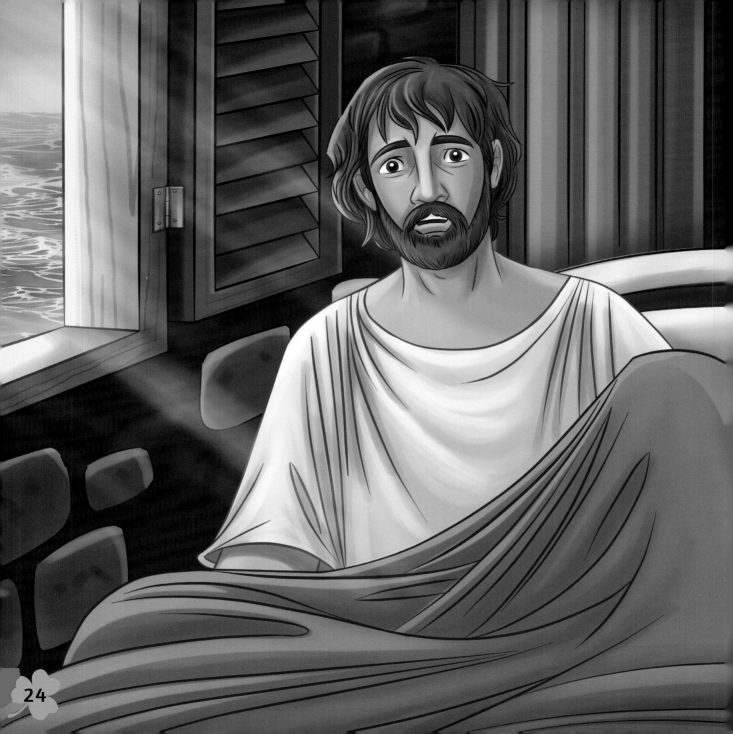

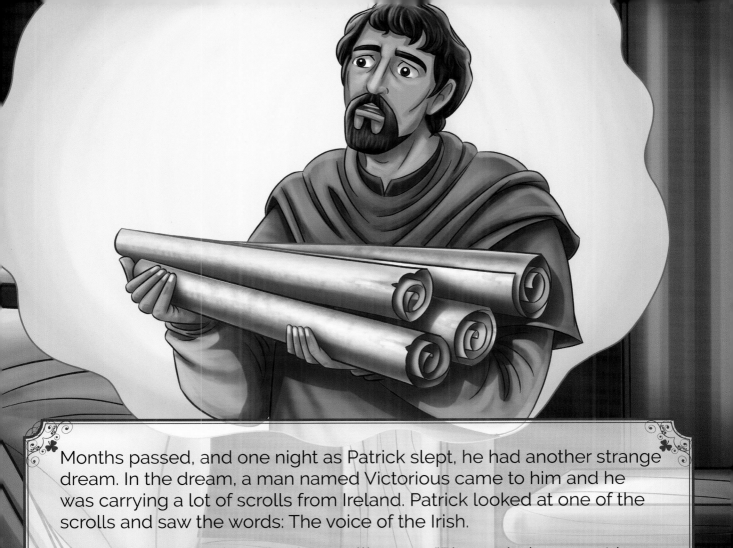

Months passed, and one night as Patrick slept, he had another strange dream. In the dream, a man named Victorious came to him and he was carrying a lot of scrolls from Ireland. Patrick looked at one of the scrolls and saw the words: The voice of the Irish.

Just then he heard voices calling out: "Please, holy servant boy, come back and walk among us!"

Patrick woke up. "God, are You asking me to go back to Ireland —the country where I was a slave?"

If the thought of going back to Ireland was difficult for Patrick, it was even more so for his parents.

"Go back?" his father pled. "But you escaped from there! They will surely kill you!"

"Please, my son!" his mother cried. "God cannot be asking you to do such a thing!"

Patrick's heart was breaking. He did not want to hurt his parents, but he knew God would work something out as He had done in the past.

"God will take care of me," he replied. "And I will not leave right away because I feel God is asking me to become a consecrated man. God is calling me to become a priest!"

Patrick left home to study. He was a very dedicated student, and after several years he was ordained a priest.

He was a faithful man and servant to God's people, and they in turn loved and respected him very much. In fact, he was such a good priest that he was made a bishop.

Patrick never forgot what God was asking him to do. He soon received permission to go as a missionary to the people of Ireland.

"What awaits me, I don't know," he said as he boarded the ship back to Ireland. "But I am sure God has a plan."

"The runaway slave is back?"

When Patrick returned to the village where he had been kept as a slave, not everyone recognized him. After all, it had been many years since his escape, and the young man had grown.

Instead, many people gathered to hear him speak about his faith. It was all a little strange to them, but some wanted to hear from the ex-slave who had returned to the land of his captivity of his own free will, even if only to satisfy their curiosity.

"Why would anyone do that?" they asked.

So Patrick took advantage of the occasion to tell them about Jesus, God's Son, who left heaven to tell sinners about God's love and forgiveness. Patrick also used a three-leaf shamrock to explain to people about the Trinity. No one in Ireland had ever heard such a thing, and some began to believe. Yet others became upset with Patrick.

"Away with him!" they yelled, picking up stones and throwing them at him. Patrick was very patient. He kept praying for the people and he continued to show them God's love. He prayed and God answered, and began to do miracles through Patrick. In fact, God did so many miracles that the Irish people started to take notice.

Many people began to accept Patrick's faith and to believe in and follow Jesus. Soon, Patrick began to set up churches throughout Ireland! The old religions of fear were soon driven away by the truth of the Christian faith!

Saint Patrick was a very courageous man. He got his courage through knowing and believing in God and His love. Prayer was the way in which Patrick came to know God. We can know God too, by spending time with Him, talking to Him in prayer and receiving the grace that He loves to give us through His Son, Jesus. Let's always remember Patrick and share his story on Saint Patrick's Day!

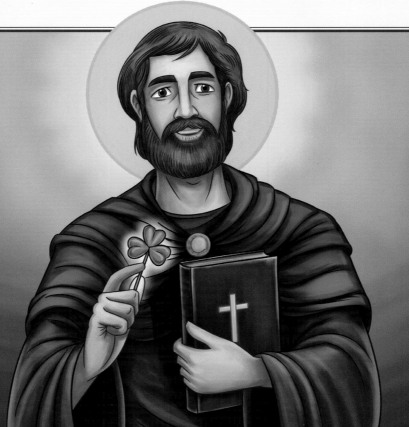

Saint Patrick wrote a prayer of faith and trust in God, a prayer well worth learning.

The Prayer of
Saint Patrick

I arise today, through
God's strength to pilot me,
God's might to uphold me,
God's wisdom to guide me,
God's eye to look before me,
God's ear to hear me,
God's word to speak for me,
God's hand to guard me,
God's shield to protect me,
God's host to save me
From snares of devils,
From temptations of vices,
From everyone who shall wish me ill,
afar and near.

Christ with me,
Christ before me,
Christ behind me,
Christ in me,
Christ beneath me,
Christ above me,
Christ on my right,
Christ on my left,
Christ when I lie down,
Christ when I sit down,
Christ when I arise,
Christ in the heart of every man who thinks of me,
Christ in the mouth of everyone who speaks of me,
Christ in every eye that sees me,
Christ in every ear that hears me.
Amen.

Enjoy your holidays with stories about the people we celebrate:

The Holiday Saints book collection!

THE STORY OF
Saint Patrick
A story of unselfish devotion

THE STORY OF
Saint Valentine
A story of courageous love

THE STORY OF
Saint Nicholas
A story of humble generosity

Stories of the people whose dedication to God
helped to change the world.

For more books like this one, visit:
www.brotherfrancisonline.com